Your Daily DOSE

(Daily Offering of Spiritual Encouragement)

by Eugene L. Jacobs

Published by Eugene L. Jacobs

I dedicate this book to the one reading these words. May you find strength and encouragement through every page.

Day 1

Genesis 22:3 (ESV)

"So Abraham rose early in the morning, saddled his donkey, and took two of his young men with him, and his son Isaac. And he cut the wood for the burnt offering and arose and went to the place of which God had told him."

Oftentimes, Abraham is praised for his faith, in that he rose early in the morning after God directed him to sacrifice the son He promised Abraham and Sarah. In fact, if the reader only reads the New Testament, Abraham seems to be the perfect example of a man walking with God. There are no flaws mentioned, none of the bad choices he made.

However, from the moment God calls Abram and throughout his life, Abraham demonstrates his humanity in the Old Testament by making some not so faithful choices. He was told to leave his kindred, but instead took his father and nephew. He was told Sarah would bear Isaac, and he agreed to "help God" with Ishmael. He withheld the truth when he said Sarah was his sister, in order to save his life.

The beautiful thing about Abraham's life, though, is that by the time we reach Genesis 22, Abraham's faith has matured. God tells Abraham to do the hardest thing he would have ever had to do, and Abraham rises early in the morning to do it. God knew when He called Abram in

Genesis 12, that Abram would not be a *perfect* man, but he would be a *perfected* man. Over time, a faulty Abram would become a faithful Abraham. As a result of his faith, we see his slate wiped clean in Romans 4:3. What a beautiful epitaph, to be remembered by God as a righteous man by faith! It was this faith that gained access to God's slate-cleaning Grace!

Abraham's story is no different than yours or mine. We all have moments of doubt. We all make choices, hoping God will bless our plans. We all make choices we feel pressured into making, not trusting God's Timing. However, Grace is right there with us through our downfalls, wiping our slates clean through our faith in Jesus! We are not the sum of our errors. For the Believer who keeps the faith, our epitaph will read (your name) believed God and was made righteous in Jesus Christ. Don't let your past cripple and label you. Get back up, keep growing, and keep going!

MY NOTES

Day 2

Psalm 77:2 (ESV)

" In the day of my trouble I seek the Lord; in the night my hand is stretched out without wearying; my soul refuses to be comforted."

Have you ever been in a season of trouble, and you cried and cried out to The Lord, but there seemed to have been no deliverance? It is in times like these, that the Believer may feel as if God has abandoned them, or that we have done something wrong and need to be punished, or that there is something to be learned and we just aren't seeing the lesson.

It's only natural for a child of God to feel as if The Lord is supposed to always deliver us from our trials and tribulations. After all, isn't that what good parents do for their children? I would like to answer in the affirmative, but the truth is sometimes good parents have to allow their children to suffer a little so that they may gain a lot more in the end.

What is our resolve, then, when we seek The Lord but can't seem to be comforted? What if God's deliverance is for us to actually endure distress? Asaph offers us a unique perspective on suffering. In Psalm 77, there seems to be no immediate relief for his pain. Asaph has done the things we normally do: pray; meditate on God's goodness;

remember what God has already done. However, Asaph says he is still overwhelmed. What was his resolve?

I'm reminded of the days when my children were much younger, when we would be in a place where they experiencedfear.Someofmyfavoritetimesweretaking them to the beach. My children were curious about the water, and wanted to venture out into it, but were afraid they might get hurt. So I took them out into the water with me. Afraid, my children didn't escape the situation, but they held tight to me. Even though they were afraid and had to endure the moment, what gave them comfort was knowing *I* wasn't afraid, and that I would not let them beharmed. Asaph'sresolveinthispsalmwasto remember that God is greater than the waters that overwhelm us. So while we may not escape whatever situation we are facing, we can hold tighter to God knowing He is greater than our problem, and He will not allow His children to be destroyed. Get a tighter grip on God's Word, on His Promises, and on His Presence.

MY NOTES

Day 3

Proverbs 18:13 (ESV)

"If one gives an answer before he hears, it is his folly and shame."

———◦◦———

Many of us have watched the scenes, where on a game show a contestant will answer wrongly before the question is asked. This, they do to try to beat the challenger to the buzzer. Many times the hurried answer will have the audience screaming with laughter. However, a quick answer is not always a joking matter.

One night, as I was driving home from class, a car came whizzing by me at an alarming speed. As the car approached a curve, I witnessed it tilt on its side, two wheels off the ground. The driver was able to correct the vehicle's posture, and the person resumed their alarming speed. Immediately I was angry. I began to hurl insults at that driver, as if they were in the car with me. As I caught up to where the driver eventually pulled off the road, I saw where they were headed in such a hurry...Their house was on fire. Imagine the shame I felt, as I had just called that person every grandmother-approved name in the book.

That night I learned to think and pray before I spoke. Yes, it still irritates me to see irrational behavior being played out on the highways, but I pray for that person and for the people they may pass along the way. I could have been hit that night. Thank God I wasn't. Someone else could have been hit. The driver could have completely flipped the car upside down. But God. Thinking *and* praying before we speak is a virtue all of us can use in every area of life; not just on the road. In our relationships and marriages, on the job, in confrontation, and in counseling others, we should learn to listen, think, and pray before we speak.

Sometimes the outward behaviors of others are a result of inward turmoil. If we are too quick to draw a conclusion about them, we may lose the opportunity to help them or even witness to them the Gospel. They may be the ones acting irrational, but we end up being the ones wearing the shame. Let us remember that we bear The Light of Christ, and if we approach matters wisely, we will be in a much better position to pray, to counsel, or to help others.

MY NOTES

Day 4

Ecclesiastes 9:18 (ESV)

"Wisdom is better than weapons of war… "

Over the years, I've heard the phrase, "it's not the cards you're dealt. It's how you play 'em." Believing myself to be a pretty good spades player(wink), I learned that phrase to hold true many times. Learning to play the game with wisdom is far more valuable than holding the right cards without knowing how and when to play them.

In Ecclesiastes 9, verses 13-16, Solomon tells of a "great king" who built "great siegeworks" against a "little city" that had "few men" in it. Pardon my intended pun, but the cards were naturally stacked against the little city. However, Solomon writes that in that little city was a poor, insignificant, unremembered man who was *wise*. By his wisdom, that poor wise man delivered that little city.

The book of Ecclesiastes reads like a collective of sayings that Solomon expresses after having learned many valuable lessons through his experience chasing vanities for so long. One of the valuable lessons he learns is that wisdom is greater than having an arsenal of weapons on your side. The wording he uses in this account purposefully paints a picture of a king who has everything and should win without question, set against the backdrop of a pushover town. However, by the end of the war, it is the poor man's wisdom that stands victorious.

Friends, be encouraged that even in your lack *or* abundance of resources, that by wisdom you can conquer kingdoms. Who you know may get you a job, but wisdom can secure promotion. What you have may afford you opportunities, but wisdom can save you time and trouble. What you know may put you in the company of experts, but pair knowledge with wisdom and you can raise a generation of experts. It's not about what you have or do not have, it's how you use what you do have, and more specifically for God's Glory.

MY NOTES

Day 5

Luke 5:12-13 (ESV)

"While he was in one of the cities, there came a man full of leprosy. And when he saw Jesus, he fell on his face and begged him, 'Lord, if you will, you can make me clean.' And Jesus stretched out his hand and touched him, saying, 'I will; be clean.' And immediately the leprosy left him."

Are you one of the many people who thought you were too far gone to be saved? Did you think you were so dirty, that you *knew* Christ wouldn't want you? In singing Amazing Grace, do you put extra emphasis on the word "wretch," as if you take ownership of the word? Do you personally argue with Paul, that *you* were the chief of sinners? You are not alone. I, too, have taken Paul to the court of my mind, arguing that I was the worst of them all.

The good news is that none of us are "too far gone." There is not one sinner that Jesus isn't willing to save. There is not one "wretch" that is so nasty that Christ isn't willing to touch with His Hand of Grace and make whole.

In our aforementioned Scripture, a man with the notoriously contagious disease of leprosy asked Jesus to heal him. However, Jesus did something above and beyond what the man asked Him to do. Jesus *touched* the man. Out of the many ways we have read Jesus heal people, surely He could have at the very least spoken a

Divine Word and healed this leper, but He *touched* him. The reason this strikes me with awe, is because to touch a leprous man was not only to become ceremonially unclean but also to risk contracting the disease. Jesus, however, has Power over all diseases and is unable to fall to any of them. So when Jesus *touches* the man, He not only shows us that He has Power over leprosy, but that He is compassionate enough to touch the untouchable.

When Jesus died on a cross on Friday, but rose early on Sunday, He proved to the world that death, hell, sin, nor the grave could conquer Him. Let this Word encourage you, Believer, that Jesus not only has Power over the sin in *your life*, but that He also is a compassionate Savior willing to touch you in your wretchedness. Let us draw near to Him, being emboldened by His ready and sure Grace and compassion, knowing that we are never too far gone to be cleansed of our spiritual leprosy-sin. Jesus *is* willing.

MY NOTES

Day 6

Hebrews 12:1 (ESV)

"Therefore, since we are surrounded by so great a cloud of witnesses, let us also lay aside every weight, and sin which clings so closely, and let us run with endurance the race that is set before us…"

Have you ever considered the fact that one of the most effective ways to lose weight is by lifting weight? Many experts say that building muscle can help turn your body into a fat burning machine. If that is the case, why don't we gain muscle by carrying around our *own* weight?

To answer that question, we need to understand that there are two different kinds of weight, healthy and unhealthy. Both weights exist for two different reasons. Gym weights are made with a purpose. Body weight is gained as a result of habits or other reasons, whether it is stress, unhealthy eating, medical reasons, etc. We carry unhealthy weight around for unhealthy reasons, and it is not the same as lifting gym weights. This kind of weight is eating away at our health.

As we consider the Text for today, one thing is obvious. Sin keeps us from effectively running the Christian race before us. However, have you ever considered the spiritually unhealthy weight in your life that keeps you from also effectively running this race? What is keeping you from being spiritually fit? From being able to endure the trials and tribulations that may come your way? What is keeping you from being able to stand under persecution and slander? From being able to resist temptation? Is it depression, or poor self-image, or lack of knowledge of Scripture or of who you are in Christ? Do you surround yourself with people who are detractors instead of investors?

Some of the things we overlook in our life, focusing only on *not sinning*, become weights that hinder us from running the race that is set before us. The writer of Hebrews specifies that our race is to be run "with endurance," meaning we have to develop the spiritual muscle to stand. He then presents Jesus as the perfect Example we are to focus on, in how Jesus endured such controversial matters in His earthly Life in order to finish the race for our benefit. How can we identify the unhealthy weight in our lives? Unhealthy weight will always result in poor performance and lack of endurance. Evaluate where you are weak, when standing on God's Word. There is where you will find the weight to be lost. Ask The Lord to help you to identify it and be rid of it. As in our natural development, we too must develop spiritual muscle to most effectively lose that weight.

MY NOTES

Day 7

Matthew 5:4 (ESV)

"Blessed are those who mourn, for they shall be comforted."

Many people are familiar with DC Comics' Superman. DC also created a character named Bizarro. Bizarro is supposed to be the "mirror image" of Superman, but he does the reverse of what Superman does. In "Bizarro World," everything is spelled backwards.

Upon reading the Beatitudes, it would seem to the reader that Jesus teaches the reverse of everything the world teaches us. Jesus seems to be the Bizarro to the world leaders' Superman. We are taught, by the world, to "get, get, get," while Jesus says, "give, give, give." We are told to be rich, while Jesus tells us to be poor. We are told to pursue happiness, while Jesus teaches us to mourn, and so forth. However, in further examination of Jesus' Sermon on the Mount, Jesus is not using the context of the world kingdoms. He is establishing the rule of His own spiritual Kingdom.

In the world, nobody wants to actually be in mourning, but in Jesus' Kingdom He salutes those who mourn. It is those who mourn that receive His Divine Comfort. What are we to mourn? Why is this a good thing in God's Eyes?

The mourning that Jesus is encouraging His disciples to partake in is grieving over our own spiritual bankruptcy. We are unable to save ourselves, and therefore it is a grievous thing to be left to our own devices. To be lifted in pride, deceiving ourselves into thinking we are virtuous by our own devices is to be rejected by God, for "He gives grace to the humble"-James 4:6. David tells us in Psalm 34:18 that, "The Lord is near to the brokenhearted and saves the crushed in spirit," and again in Psalm 51:17, "the sacrifices of God are a broken spirit; a broken and contrite heart, O God, you will not despise."

It is wise and vital for the disciple to take the "Bizarro" route and live opposite the world. The world teaches us to be proud of who we are, sinful nature and all. Jesus teaches us to despise our sinful nature. Then, and only then, will we receive the comfort of His Grace and Mercy. We cannot be made righteous through our own efforts to perform for God. It is only by His Grace, paired with our faith in Jesus' Blood sacrifice, that we are truly made righteous.

MY NOTES

Day 8

Psalm 3:1-3 (ESV)

" O LORD, how many are my foes! Many are rising against me; many are saying of my soul, there is no salvation for him in God. Selah. But you, O LORD, are a shield about me, my glory, and the lifter of my head. "

Undoubtedly, David had many occasions where his life was in danger and he had to rely on the salvation of The Lord. Before he fought in his first war, he had to defend his father's sheep from a lion and a bear. He, while still young and not yet formally trained for battle, stood against the giant of Gath. While he was serving in the court of King Saul, he fled for his life from the very king he was called to minister to. In the Scripture for today, David is now fleeing his own son, Absalom, who believes he is a better fit for the throne than his father. Absalom has won the heart of many, having stood in the gates to hear their issues. He is considered a handsome man with long, flowy hair. When David pens this psalm, he writes as though his enemies(those of his own kin) have increased and have already counted him out. However, he remembers the same God that has been with him through the entirety of his life.

Beloved, people may have counted you out. You may have even given up on yourself, due to the circumstances around you. Remember this, though. God for you is more than the world against you. He is our Divine Protector, Comforter, and Savior. Even though you and I have to endure some storms in our lives, know that God is our constant support. He loves His children.

He sees when our heads are hung in shame and despair, and He is the lifter up of our heads. It has been said for many years that "storms won't last always." Our Lord is a shelter in the very midst of every storm. Will you trust Him today?

MY NOTES

Day 9

1 John 2:1 (ESV)

*"My little children, I am writing these things to you so that
you may not sin. But if anyone does sin, we have an
Advocate with the Father, Jesus Christ the righteous."*

———◆———

I can recount many occasions where I needed comfort, whether
it be a financial need, medical assistance, or emotional support.
Receiving comfort during these times was truly a blessing, but
when the situation was handled, I needed no further comfort.

Considering our Text for today, the apostle John encourages us
of a comfort we Believers can always rely on...the comfort of
always being able to rely on our Advocate. True Believers never
want to return to a life of sin, much less sin at all. In his epistle,
John tells us *not* to sin, *but* if we *do*, we have an Advocate with
God The Father in Jesus Christ The Son.

What does it mean to have an "advocate?" The Greek word
used here means an intercessor or consoler. It's the same word
Jesus used when He said He would send us another Comforter.
Jesus doesn't just simply make us *feel better*. He intercedes for
us through His already shed Blood. Every sin we have and will
ever commit is covered in The Blood of Jesus. Now, this isn't a
license to sin. Once again, John stated that he wrote his epistle
so that we would not sin. However, in our fallen human bodies,
The Believer is still prone to error. In the case of those errors,
we can appeal to Jesus to afford us the sure mercies of The
Father because He lived sin*less* to present us *spot*less. Knowing

this gives me comfort every day. Because of Jesus I, once being in enmity with God, now have peace with God. Thank God for Jesus!

MY NOTES

Day 10

Hebrews 10:19-20 (ESV)

"Therefore, brothers...we have confidence to enter the Holy places by The Blood of Jesus, by the new and living way that He opened for us through the curtain, that is, through His Flesh,

———❖———

Under the Old Testament Law, only the Levitical high priest could enter the sacred Holiest of Holies, where the Ark of the Covenant rested. Atonement for the sins of Israel rested on the work of the high priest in that holy Place. If the high priest did not perform as commanded, not only was his life in danger, but the people would still stand unatoned for. Wouldn't it be a scary thing to place, essentially, your entire life in the hands of a man capable of failing?

Fast forward to the New Testament, after Jesus has died on a cross and rose again. The writer of Hebrews tells us that Jesus fulfilled the roles of our Sacrifice, High Priest, and Substitute. It is because of this that Jesus has prepared the Believer to enter a place he/she was once forbidden and, if permitted, would have entered in fear. We can entrust our very lives in The Perfect Hands of Jesus. The writer doesn't say that only the high priest can enter the Holiest of Holies. The writer says "we have confidence!" We! Every Believer can approach The Presence of God without fear of failure! Jesus has opened to us access to the very Holy Presence that condemns the sinner through His own Flesh that was pierced for us! Think about that for a minute. Without Jesus, we are denied access. *Through* Jesus, regardless of the sin stains we once wore, we enter into The Presence of God covered by His Blood where we now obtain mercy. Oh, what a Savior! We don't just stand *before* God's Presence…We stand *in* His Presence.

MY NOTES

Day 11

Proverbs 20:4 (ESV)

"The sluggard does not plow in the autumn; he will seek at harvest and have nothing."

————⟡————

The King James Version reads, "the sluggard will not plow by reason of the cold…" Do you have goals? Do you know what it takes to achieve those goals? Have you begun taking the steps toward achieving those goals, or are you making excuses? I have often said that making excuses is a creative way to reject thetruth. Thetruthis,ifyouwanttoachievethegoalsyouhave set for yourself, you're going to have to be willing to do some things you might not feel like doing.

In today's Scripture, we find an example of what we could call a procrastinator, or a "slow poke." This individual wants to reap at harvest time, but doesn't want to put in the work when he should because of the weather. Sounds preposterous, doesn't it? A farmer wants a field of apples, but doesn't want to put in the work to plant the seeds. However preposterous that may seem, many of us follow his example.

Do you want to lose weight, but don't want to quit your eating habits or exercise? Do you want to have money in the bank, but don't want to put in the work or change your spending habits? Do you want a happy home, but are unwilling to change your perspectives on things in order to make peace and resolve disagreements? Do you want your children to behave, but make excuses for why you can't discipline them? Do you want a closer walk with Jesus, but make excuses for why you can't attend any of the teaching avenues instituted by your local church? It's preposterous to expect results when you reject the work needed to produce them.

Don't make excuses. Accept that it's going to take some sacrifices to achieve the results you want. Don't be a sluggard.

MY NOTES

Day 12

Numbers 23:11-12 (ESV)

"And Balak said to Balaam, 'What have you done to me? I took you to curse my enemies, and behold, you have done nothing but bless them.' And he answered and said, 'Must I not take care to speak what the LORD puts in my mouth?'"

———◇———

Have you ever found yourself the victim of someone else's verbal assaults, having been insulted and even had "hexes" cast at you? People can say pretty mean and outlandish things to us when they can't have their way with us. Some even go as far as actually believing they can put a curse upon our lives. What about long held superstitions? Do you believe in the curses embraced by many superstitious people?

In the Scripture for today Balak, king of the Moabites, is set on cursing the Israelites by way of a man who practiced divination named Balaam. Four times Balak is disappointed, due to the fact that every time Balaam opens his mouth to curse Israel he blesses them instead. Why? God wouldn't allow it. It was The King of all Creation putting words of blessing in Balaam's mouth instead of the words of curses the earthly king of Moab told Balaam to speak that prevailed.

I want to encourage you today, that what God has blessed, no man nor devil can curse. There is no hex, superstition, nor urban legend that can befall you when God's Hand of blessing is onyou. Eventoday,onestillseesthefearofsuperstition dominate the thinking and actions of others, Believers included.

There are no split poles, jinxes, speaking the same things at the same times, broken mirrors, black cats, wrong sides of coins, nor any other superstitions that can overturn the Power of God in our lives! If you are a child of God, you are kept by Him! Cast off that old way of thinking. Even if it seems like you're cursed because of circumstances in your life, I want to tell you that you are not. The only curse that holds power over an individual is the curse of Adam on the entire race of mankind, broken by Jesus Christ and those who believe on Him.

So today, I won't close with a "God bless you" or a "be blessed." Walk in the blessedness of Jesus today. You're already blessed!

MY NOTES

Day 13

Luke 15:31 (ESV)

"And he said to him, 'Son, you are always with me, and all that is mine is yours…"

Have you ever bought milk, planning to soon use it with your cereal, oatmeal, or recipe only to forget it was there? Perhaps you finally got the strong craving to sit down to a nice bowl of cereal for a late snack, opened the refrigerator, began to break the seal on the milk jug, and found the milk had gone sour and out of date. Were you disappointed like I was? It's a sour occasion (pardon the pun) to have a good thing and let it go to waste.

The son in our aforementioned Text was sour because his father threw a great feast, welcoming his other son back home. The son being celebrated, as many know, wasted the inheritance he demanded from his father but later returned home asking his father to receive him as a servant. If it were up to his sour brother, he may not have even gotten the chance to return to the estate at all. However, his father welcomed him with open arms and refused his request to become a servant, instead restoring him as a son. The sour brother retorted, saying he had always stayed on his father's estate but never received a celebration. His father's response is beautiful and yet goes unappreciated by many. "You are always with me, and all that is mine is yours…" In other words, if the sour son wanted or needed anything, it was already his to have. The wealth of the entire estate was his to share and enjoy.

Do you find yourself scowling at the people you don't believe deserve to be blessed, wondering why you don't have what they have? That's called covetousness, by the way. The Believer has no need to worry about what others have when we already are joint-heirs with Christ. Do you not appreciate the fact that you are the child of The Lord of all Creation, or do you not truly realize it? Has "the milk been on the shelf" the whole time while you ignore it? Don't let your "milk sour." Follow the Words of Jesus in Matthew 6:33, "But seek ye first The Kingdom of God, and His Righteousness; and all these things shall be added unto you."

MY NOTES

Day 14

Psalm 29:4 (ESV)

"The Voice of The LORD is powerful; The Voice of The LORD is full of majesty."

Psalm 29 is interesting because seven times David mentions The Voice of God, drawing encouragement. What is so significant about God's Voice that should encourage us today? Everything. Our words can encourage, hurt, destroy, grant access, and even define a thing. However, God's Words bring manifestation. When God spoke, Creation was formed of nothing. When God spoke, prophecies became realities. When God spoke, His Covenant bound Him to keep His Word. The gospel of John tells us that God's Word even became flesh! You see, whatever God speaks can only be undone by Him. What He says must come to pass, because He is God.

Wondering about salvation? Trust what God said, and not what man adds. Wondering if He still heals? Trust God's Word. Wondering about what direction to take in life? Trust God's Word. He will direct your paths. Many times, we want quick fixes in life, or we want God to speak a new Word over our lives, but God has already spoken what we need to hear. Find it in His Word. God's Word wins wars and gives life at the same time. His Word brings judgment and justice as well as wrath and vengeance. His Word destroys nations while commanding gentle breezes. He commands storms and holds the ocean back with His Word. Don't underestimate The Power of God's Voice.

MY NOTES

Day 15

Isaiah 40:31 (ESV)

"But they who wait for the LORD shall renew their strength; they shall mount up with wings like eagles; they shall run and not be weary; they shall walk and not faint."

How often have you poured all your effort and strength into doing good, and being faithful, and trying to keep things afloat only to see matters get worse? Now, be honest with yourself. Did you really seek The Lord before you poured all your effort into those things, or did you just ask God to bless the things you were doing? I've been a bird enthusiast since I was four years old, identifying the birds in our backyard with my mother. I am amazed at the colors, the calls, and the different types of birds that fill the air, but there are two birds of the same family that have always caught my eye...hawks and eagles. While other birds spend great energy flapping their wings to go great distances, hawks and eagles rely on the wind and soar to greater heights than smaller birds. Research has shown that hawks and eagles spend 50-90% less energy soaring than smaller birds do flying. They literally ride the wind.

Isaiah writes, "but they who wait for The Lord...shall mount up with wings like eagles." The idea here isn't just to have wings, but "wings like eagles." When we wait patiently for The Lord to lead us in His Timing, we don't have to spend so much energy trying to get things to work on our own. God is the One carrying us. This is not to say you don't have to put forth any effort or that there won't be a struggle at all, but waiting for The Lord and relying on His Will makes our struggles so much easier. You'll be able to run and not be weary and walk without becoming faint. In other words, waiting on God and riding on the winds of His Power will carry us to infinitely greater heights and distances without relying on our own efforts. Stop struggling. Wait on The Lord.

MY NOTES

Day 16

James 1:2-4 (ESV)

"Count it all joy, my brothers, when you meet trials of various kinds, for you know that the testing of your faith produces steadfastness. And let steadfastness have its full effect, that you may be perfect and complete, lacking in nothing."

I don't know anyone who joyfully sends out invitations for trials and tribulations. Suffering is probably the last thing on your bucket list. As a matter of fact, you're probably verbally saying it's not even on your bucket list. James, however, tells us to "count it all joy" when we suffer trials and tribulations. How odd a statement is that?

I was inspired once to say, in a sermon, that God loves us too much to just be in the business of making us comfortable. If He was that kind of God, all of His children would be spoiled brats. Pardon my saying. If we had our way, all of us would be rich, never sick, and would continue living until Jesus came back for us. However, having things go that way would leave us spiritually empty. It's God's Will for us to be like Him, not just for our own good, but so that we can be His ambassadors-ministers of reconciliation that witness to the world. The Lord knows that it is far more important for us to be perfected spiritually than it is for us to be comfortable naturally.

How can we count "trials of various kinds" as all joy? Our will must line up with God's Will. When that happens, we can rejoice in the fact that God is allowing patience to have her perfecting work on us, bringing us into the Christlikeness we so desire to emulate. God is working all things together for good for those of us who love Him. Are you willing to be shaped by The Potter?

MY NOTES

Day 17

Matthew 11:28-30 (ESV)

"Come to me, all who labor and are heavy laden, and I will give you rest. Take my yoke upon you, and learn from me, for I am gentle and lowly in heart, and you will find rest for your souls. For my yoke is easy, and my burden is light."

I love to see hard-working individuals celebrate their retirement. Giving twenty to fifty plus years faithfully to any institution is an accomplishment to be celebrated indeed. The best part about seeing an individual retire, to me, is seeing the look of rest and peace on their faces in the aftermath. No more getting up early every day if you choose. No more fighting through illness to save your PTO. No more dealing with attitudes, or putting off important family events, or sudden changes at work, or working in spite of pain, etc. Being able to rest is a blessing.

For some of us, rest seems almost sinful. I remember being on a minister's retreat where we were told we would be served from the time we pulled up to the cabin until the time we left. That is literally what happened, too. For the first 2 days, I couldn't stop fighting the urge to do the things others were trying to do for me. It just wasn't necessary to me. These were things I do on a daily basis. After being emphatically told to stop and rest about 30 times (lol), I finally gave in. By the end of the retreat, I learned what a blessing and a privilege it is to finally get some rest.

Friends, Jesus did the work of procuring our salvation through His Blood so we can enter into God's rest. However, many of us keep reverting back to our old ways of trying to "fix" ourselves through means of law. Trying to earn salvation through works is like devoting your whole life to working an assembly line job without ever getting paid, except we do get paid...The wages of sin is death. If we work to earn salvation, we are never free from sin and therefore never saved. Jesus is gracefully inviting us into retirement from our tireless and unfruitful labor. He has done all the work to cleanse us from sin. Receive that truth by faith and enjoy the fruit of His labor...rest.

MY NOTES

Day 18

Proverbs 3:5-6 (ESV)

"Trust in the LORD with all your heart, and do not lean on your own understanding. In all your ways acknowledge him, and he will make straight your paths."

Gaining knowledge and understanding is a good thing. Even the Bible tells us, "in all our getting, get an understanding." However, the context of knowledge and understanding must be understood biblically. Proverbs 1:7 says, "the fear of The LORD is the beginning of knowledge…" Where we get into trouble is with the knowledge that comes outside this context. When it comes to life, many of us rely on our knowledge and understanding of how things naturally occur, but we apply those same principles to how our supernatural God is supposed to operate in our lives. If we need bills paid, we expect for God to provide money. If we need healing, we expect for God to show the doctor what's wrong with us and either medicate or operate. If we need comfort, we expect for God to surround us with people who sympathize with us. Leaning to our own understanding will cause us to overlook God cancelling a bill, or miraculously healing us, or comforting us supernaturally in the silence of privacy.

If you're going to trust God with "all your heart," you're going to have to believe that The Lord is able to accomplish what naturally cannot be accomplished. He is able to miraculously solve your problems and He is able to supernaturally guide you through the natural means of getting your problems solved. How will you know which path God has for you to take? "In all your ways acknowledge him, and he will make straight your paths." That's the answer. The Word teaches us to pray about *everything*. I usually tell people I even pray about what grocery store to go to and what things to buy. You never know when God will lead you to witness to an individual in front of frozen food. If God is going to cancel your bill, He will. If God leads you to call the bill collector and ask for help, God will walk with you through the phone call and work the situation out for you. You've got to acknowledge Him first and always. His Word says, "and He *will* direct (or make straight) your paths."

MY NOTES

Day 19

Hebrews 13:8 (ESV)

"Jesus Christ is the same yesterday and today and forever."

The world in which we live has increasingly become a hotbed of division. The things people disagree on are not just topics of debate anymore. People have taken action, including violence against those who don't think the way they do. The realm of Christianity is no different in the 21st Century. There are so many differences between the people representing Jesus that the world is confused. At times, it's discouraging to see "Christians" who are bigots, "Christians" who are greedy, "Christians" who worship worldly leaders, "Christians" who try to control others through the Bible, "Christians" who lack grace and compassion, and the list goes on. Some people have dared make videos on the internet saying they left their religion because of "Christians" like this, somehow believing this is the way all Believers behave.

If you find yourself discouraged these days, let me help bring you back to focus. Regardless of how many human beings represent and misrepresent Jesus, our Savior remains the same. He's not hiding. His Person and Character shine brightly throughout the pages of Scripture. He is, has always been, and always will be consistently Jesus. It's Him we must discover, and learn, and emulate. Not others, unless they're actually following the Jesus of the Bible. "Follow me as I follow Christ."

How does this encourage me? I'm glad you asked. Knowing Jesus is the same yesterday, today, and forever lets me know that He is not the brutes we see on television, nor is He no less powerful or impactful than He was in the Bible. We're not dealing with anything new. The present day we are living is history repeating itself, and the influences of the world then could not snuff out His Light. Just cling to the Jesus of the Bible. Learn of Him. Emulate Him. Show and tell others about Him. Let His Light shine through you so men may see your good works and glorify our Heavenly Father. Stay consistent. Keep the faith. God sees what's going on today, and He knows the answer is still Jesus...the TRUE Jesus. Even in this divisive climate, Jesus is still in the soul-saving business.

MY NOTES

Day 20

Isaiah 26:3 (ESV)

"You keep him in perfect peace whose mind is stayed on you, because he trusts in you."

———◦◦◦———

How many times have you prayed about something and the situation didn't change? Did you do like I used to do and begin to worry yourself into a panic attack? When studying this Scripture for a sermon, a thought was planted in my spirit…"Prayer might not change the situation, but it changes Who is handling the situation." It's the Who we need to trust and not the circumstances. God spoke through Isaiah to a nation that had been oppressed by an enemy who had committed heinous acts. It seemed like there was no hope for Judah. The circumstances spelled out certain doom for them. However, God breaks through the dark clouds with a ray of hope through His Word assuring them they could trust *Him.*

Let me remind you that The Name of The Lord is a strong tower, and that God is our refuge, and that His Salvation fortifies us against the worst of enemies-even death. When your circumstances are unsteady, steady your mind on thoughts of The Lord. He will keep you in "perfect peace." When I'm going through trials, I try not to focus on my situation. I focus on the God who is able to fix my situation. Even if my situation doesn't change, I rest in the truth that God is working all things out for my good, and He is with me.

MY NOTES

Day 21

Galatians 6:9 (ESV)

"And let us not grow weary of doing good, for in due season we will reap, if we do not give up."

———❖———

The world teaches us that what goes around comes around. It's called karma. That's not necessarily always true. Many times you do for others and it seems like they go on to prosper while you suffer one hit after another. Scripture teaches us a spiritual law, though, that sounds similar to karma but is not karma. It's the law of planting and harvesting. It works in a similar way to natural farming. What you plant comes up, *if* you're consistent to plant, and water, and do maintenance on what you've planted. Naturally,the fruit that is produced is according to the seed that is planted. No one plants an apple seed and harvests a plum tree. You may have come across this Scripture and taken it on as a life verse. When good things happen to you, you reference this "life verse," and say it's because of Galatians 6:9. But what do you do when you've done so much for a person or for people and nothing comes back to you? Does the same "life verse" still apply?

Let me help you look at this Text in a different light. First, why are you doing good? Is it because you want God to give you back more than you gave others? Do you look at people as savings accounts you pour into, hoping God will add interest and let you draw from them later? If this is the case, your motives are wrong. We are to be consistent in doing good works because Jesus told His disciples to let His Light in us shine so men will glorify God when they see the works we do. Ephesians 2 says we are created in Christ Jesus for good works. We've been enabled to do the work that glorifies and honors God. So our focus is to live lives that point others to The Lord, period. There are no strings to be attached to our service to God. It does get discouraging and tiring to be consistent in giving and not receiving at the same rate. This is why Paul encourages us to not "grow weary of doing good…" It doesn't mean you won't get tired or discouraged. It means not to give up due to being tired and/or discouraged. And when the season for harvesting comes for you, it's your season. There's no stopping it. What you've sowed consistently will give way to a harvest because that's the law of sowing and reaping. Just don't sow because you expect to reap. Sow to honor The Lord.

MY NOTES

Day 22

1 Thessalonians 5:16-18 (ESV)

"Rejoice always, pray without ceasing, give thanks in all circumstances; for this is the will of God in Christ Jesus for you."

I've been in many situations where I don't feel like giving thanks. When your car breaks down, you don't feel too thankful. When you've been abused and neglected, you don't feel so thankful. When you're broke and need to feel your family, you don't feel so grateful. When your husband, wife, or significant other leaves you and your kids to fend for yourselves, you might not feel like giving thanks. Scripture says, though, to give thanks "in all circumstances." How is one supposed to give thanks when it seems their world is falling apart?

Always remember that you aren't the first person to go through trials and tribulations. Paul and the other apostles of the New Testament wrote to Believers who were being persecuted and killed for their faith in Jesus Christ. We in America have never seen the government persecute us for what we believe. For those who offer a rebuttal to the statement I just made, compare yourselves to the receiving audience of the epistles of the apostles. The writer of Hebrews highlights just a few things the early Christians faced in Chapter 11. If those Believers were encouraged to give thanks in all circumstances, surely we have much to be thankful for.

The problem comes when we become entitled, thinking God is supposed to give us everything we want-seeing our wants as "needs." In order to be thankful, we have to be able to see the benefits of being a child of God. Paul said that God is working all things together "for good for those who love God and are the called, according to His purpose." Therefore, even when my situation doesn't clearly spell out the silver lining in the clouds, we still know that God is bringing the good out of it and is bringing us to a place of His expectations. At the end of the day, life on this earth and in this flesh will come with its challenges, but God has ultimately promised us eternal life and immortal bodies. I am thankful for His promises and for salvation alone. We all have earned the wages of sin, but in Christ are given the gift of God. So, in everything, we have much to be thankful for.

MY NOTES

Day 23

James 4:7-8 (ESV)

"Submit yourselves therefore to God. Resist the devil, and he will flee from you. Draw near to God, and he will draw near to you."

For decades, I've heard people quote, "resist the devil and he will flee." Holding to this quote, without studying the actual Scripture, I made it my aim to fight to resist the devil. I'm sure many people did the same as I, fighting with all their might to make the devil run from them due to their resistance to temptation. The problem is, not only is that not the entire verse, but this ideology causes the Believer to fight a spiritual battle through physical means. That's a battle that cannot be won. How many people have said they wanted to "go to church" as soon as they get themselves together? I've heard many say that and then never show up "to church" because they fail to get themselves together.

Friend, the Scripture gives us the key to resisting the devil in the first and last sentences. "Submit yourselves therefore to God...Draw near to God..." When I see the word "therefore," I always look at what was said before we got "there." James tells us that the fleshly spirit is something else to deal with, but God supplies more grace. God resists the proud, but gives grace to the humble. Therefore, when temptation arises, don't just start a Just Say No campaign against the devil. Submit to God. Draw near to Him. Feel the warmth of His all-sufficient grace. It's a losing battle to just focus on fighting the devil. We wrestle not against flesh and blood. Submitting to God begins with the acknowledgement that you need Him and cannot depend on yourself for this spiritual battle. You are spiritually bankrupt without Him, but by His grace, you are loved and welcomed by Him. Focusing on the devil alone leaves you to the thoughts of failure he always plants in your head. He wants you to surrender to him due to your inability to win against him. "You might as well stay in (sin) because this is who you are." But God's grace fills in the gaps in your character and life. He loves you so much. Hear His affirmations of you in His Word. Let God's grace dispel the lies of Satan. You are forgiven. You are His. You are accepted in the Beloved. You are more than a conqueror. Nothing can separate you from His Love. You have overcome by The Blood of The Lamb and the word of your testimony. You are filled with The Spirit that has defeated all demonic spirits. You don't have to sin, because that's not who you are. You have been freed from sin and are free to walk in the newness of life in Christ Jesus. Amen.

MY NOTES

Day 24

Luke 1:78-79 (ESV)

"...because of the tender mercy of our God, whereby the sunrise shall visit us from on high to give light to those who sit in darkness and in the shadow of death, to guide our feet into the way of peace."

I'm a steak man. I love to sit down to a nice and juicy, well-seasoned, tender steak! When the knife slides through a thick steak like it's butter, I know I'm about to have a good meal. Now that I've made you hungry, let me tell you why I mentioned steak. The steak isn't the subject of the encouragement today. The tenderness is today's subject. When something is tender, it's been softened to a certain degree of pleasantry.

God's Heart might not be something you put on a plate to enjoy, but It sure is tender toward a people who deserve nothing but cold and callous condemnation. In the Text today, The Holy Spirit speaks to God's tender mercy through the father of John the Baptist. These words are poetic to me. Through these words, Jesus is being called the S-U-N that rose in the middle of the night. The KJV calls Him "the dayspring from on high," and the ESV calls Jesus simply, "the sunrise." To a world that sat in darkness because of sin, God mercifully supplied us with The Light of Life. Did we deserve it? No. The wages of sin is death. We all earned our place in eternal condemnation. But God's mercy is so tender; He couldn't leave us without providing us a way out of condemnation and into Eternal Life.

Can you imagine laying down in your bed at midnight and seeing the windows brighten with the light of the sun, hearing the birds chirping and the roosters crowing as if it were 7:00 am? That's what God did for us through Jesus Christ, except midnight was a time of terror and judgement and not a time to lay down and enjoy rest and the shining light, the Life flooding a world filled with death. I appreciate the tenderness of God's Heart so much. I am the beneficiary of His tender mercies which are renewed daily. God looked beyond my faults and supplied my needs. Thank you, Lord!

MY NOTES

Day 25

2 Corinthians 5:8 (ESV)

"Yes, we are of good courage, and we would rather be away from the body and at home with the Lord."

———※———

Ever since I was a child, I heard people speak these words in conversation and in prayer, "Thank God I woke up on this side of the earth." I've heard people say, "I'd rather been seen than viewed." I've also heard people say, "I'm so thankful my bed wasn't my cooling board." This might not seem like the kind of encouragement you wanted to read today, thoughts of death, but I'd like to help adjust your perspective.

Scripture teaches us that being away from these earthly bodies, which are fading away, equates to us being "at Home with The Lord." Nowadays, when I hear people repeat the aforementioned phrases, I kindly rebuttal with, "either way I'm with The Lord." The Believer must normalize being okay with letting go of the world. In John 11, Jesus told Lazarus' sister Martha, "I am The Resurrection and The Life. If any man believes in Me, though he were dead, yet shall he live. And whosoever lives and believes in me shall never die." These words should encourage us today. Death is never the fate of the Believer. Jesus experienced and conquered our death so that we would never have to experience it. We think about the things and people we'll miss, but will we miss them or will they miss us? I think it's the other way around. We will be in Eternal Joy and Rest with The Lord. I read a short story about a water bug that made a pact with his friends. Every day, they'd see a water bug climb up a stem to the surface of the water and never return. The friends made a pact that if one of them ever climbed to the surface, they'd come back and tell the others what was so great about the surface. One day, the little water bug had a strong urge within, tugging at him to climb to the surface of the water. When he got above the water, he noticed he had wings among other changes to his body. He flew around and enjoyed his new equipment. Then, he thought about his pact with his friends and tried to return back underwater to tell about his new and thrilling experience. However, he was unable to return underwater. He had become a dragonfly. He thought to himself, "I can't keep my promise, but someday they'll see for themselves how much better it is up here."

Perhaps this encouragement is for you to find closure with the ones you've grieved over. Your beloved didn't "lose their battle" with cancer, or dementia, or with any other condition of the human experience. If they left here a Believer, they never died. They never lost. In Christ, your beloved *and you* have won the victory over death. Be encouraged. God bless you.

MY NOTES

Romans 8:38-39 (ESV)

"For I am sure that neither death nor life, nor angels nor rulers, nor things present nor things to come, nor powers, nor height nor depth, nor anything else in all creation, will be able to separate us from the love of God in Christ Jesus our Lord."

I chuckle sometimes when I reminisce about the "love songs" of the past. It seems like everybody wanted to cross the oceans, the deserts, offer the sun, moon, and stars, and climb mountains to prove their love to the object of their affections. Promises of never lying, cooking, cleaning, rubbing feet, and loving you like nobody else could, filled the airwaves every day through music. People can be fickle, though. We make the grandest promises, but the smallest disturbances cause the biggest of breakups. How many factors change our love for one another? Whether it was the wrong look, or one "woke up on the wrong side of the bed," or one is having a bad day, or one doesn't "feel well," or trials come, we've all had a tendency to break a promise or two to love like no other, due to circumstances.

Even though we humans can be impressive serenading one another, no one compares to our God in His expression of love toward us. God means what He says, and He performs what He says He will perform. He spends no time speaking idle words, hoping to win us over. He loves us unconditionally. There are no disturbances that will alter His love for us. The list of potential disturbances found in Romans 8 are no match for the love of God. These potential obstacles eclipse the promises singers croon over: tribulation, distress, persecution, famine, nakedness, peril, sword, death, life, angels, rulers, nothing present or future, powers, height, depth, nor anything you can think of in all of Creation. Nothing...absolutely *nothing* will alter how God loves you. His grace, mercy, deliverance, forgiveness, all of the benefits of God's love will always be available to you because Jesus Christ has made us joint-heirs of His Inheritance. Nobody else can love you like that. So,when you feel let down by the inconsistency of mankind's love, remember that you are perfectly and unconditionally loved already.

MY NOTES

Day 27

Jude 24-25 (ESV)

"Now to him who is able to keep you from stumbling and to present you blameless before the presence of his glory with great joy, to the only God, our Savior, through Jesus Christ our Lord, be glory, majesty, dominion, and authority, before all time and now and forever. Amen."

It can be overwhelming sometimes, thinking about how flawed we are and how many times we do the wrong things. Some days, I feel terrible for the things I did in the past. I often wonder and ask The Lord how He could love a person like me, much less wash all my sins away. Our Scripture for today reminds us that in Christ, God is able to keep us from stumbling *and* make us blameless before His Holy Presence. Think about that.

First, we are being kept stable. After Peter made his faith confession that Jesus is The Christ, The Son of The Living God, Jesus told him He would build His Church upon The Solid Rock that is Jesus and our faith in Him. "On Christ, The Solid Rock I stand; all other ground is sinking sand." Standing on Jesus by faith keeps us from falling back into a state of sin. He lives forever, making intercession for those of us who trust Him. John said for us not to sin, but when we do, we have an advocate with The Father, Jesus Christ The Righteous. God has us covered, standing firmly on The One who sanctifies us and clothes us with righteousness and Salvation.

Secondly, to *know* we sinned and desired to do so, but still be presented blameless before God seems like a trick. Is God bamboozled? Does He not know how much wrong we've done? God knows, indeed! Jude didn't say we *are* blameless, but that we are *presented* blameless. It was always God's plan for His people to use blood to atone for their sins. The blood of the innocent was exchanged for the bloodguiltiness of the sinner. A substitute paid the penalty for the guilty. God isn't tricked into not seeing our guilt. Jesus became our Substitute willingly and shed His Blood, the just for the unjust that our penalty would fall on Him. What a Savior! One of my favorite Scriptures is 2 Corinthians 5:21 - "For he hath made him to be sin for us, who knew no sin; that we might be made the righteousness of God in him." It sounds unfair, but that's the love of God.

It amazes me that one day, the Believer will be able to stand before a God, who's holiness alone condemns everything that isn't spotless, in the same manner Adam and Eve once did in the garden. Not because we were born perfect and stayed perfect, but we will be able to do so because in being born *again*, Christ has graced us to put on *His* perfection. We will stand before God naked and unashamed...exposed, but unflawed. What a blessing!

MY NOTES

Day 28

Ephesians 3:20-21 (ESV)

"Now to him who is able to do far more abundantly than all that we ask or think, according to the power at work within us, to him be glory in the church and in Christ Jesus throughout all generations, forever and ever. Amen."

Little children are so funny and impressionable. I like to play with them and make them think I'm the strongest man in the world. They run up to one item after another and ask, "can you pick this up?" I like to make a show of it, grunting and pretending to struggle until I lift the item in victory. I know you can imagine their little faces, as many of you have probably done the same thing. Their requests are so simple, but because they haven't been exposed to much, their imaginations have only been stretched so far.

We are like that with God. Sometimes we limit God to our own imaginations. Paul says that The Lord is able to do "far more abundantly than *all* we ask or think." We approach God like, "can you lift this burden," when we should know He is more than able to. Is there anything too hard for God? That's a rhetorical question, by the way. There is nothing too hard for God besides failing and sinning.

Don't miss this part, though. Paul says, "according to the Power at work within us." Now, we know God can do anything outside of us, but do you believe He is able to accomplish more than you can imagine *from within*? When you lay hands on the sick, do you doubt the Power at work within you? When you walk into new spaces, do you doubt the Power at work within you? When you've been asked to speak before an audience or congregation, do you doubt the ability of the Power at work within you? When faced with temptations, do you doubt the Power at work within you? The same God who is at work apart from you is the same Spirit at work from within you. Don't doubt or limit Him. He is more than able.

MY NOTES

Day 29

2 Corinthians 13:14 (ESV)

"The grace of the Lord Jesus Christ and the love of God and the fellowship of the Holy Spirit be with you all."

These are words I quote at the end of service every Sunday morning. They are the words I heard the wise man who pastored me for most of my life say for the benediction every Sunday. Why are these words worth remembering and repeating? This doxology carries a threefold blessing: grace, love, and fellowship.

I like to define grace as God heaping on us blessings we don't deserve and can never earn. Grace is one powerful attribute. In Scripture, we see grace carrying us when we are weak, granting us the gifting of The Holy Spirit, extending to us the free gift of Salvation, and creating us anew among other things. Jesus' substitutionary death on the cross opened the door for us to receive this heaping of the blessings of God.

As you've read in a previous devotional entry, there is nothing that can alter the Love of God toward His children. Jesus said there is no greater love than a man laying down his life for his friends. I always say that Jesus laid down His Life so that His enemies could be His friends. Having the Love of God ensures me that God won't turn away from me because I don't deserve His Love. He is faithful and He is just to forgive.

Then, there is this fellowship piece. I don't know anyone who really wants to *always* be alone. I've been a loner for all my life.

I've just never had a desire to have a large company of friends and associates around me. I like my solitude, and I like to think and not hear other voices in my ears, but there are times I really appreciate having good fellowship with friends and family. The fellowship is warm, encouraging, affirming, and loving. Fellowship with The Person of God and Christ through The Holy Spirit is so much more than fellowship with friends and family. I have the counsel of God, the Power of God, the revelation of God, the correction of God, the ever-affirming promises of God with me. His Spirit bears witness with my spirit that I am His and He is my Father. The noise of Satan's accusations is silenced by the fellowship I have with The Holy Spirit.

No matter how tough situations may get, knowing I have God's grace, love, and fellowship through Jesus keeps me encouraged. I pray it does for you as well from now until forever. God bless you.

MY NOTES

Day 30

1 Peter 5:10-11 (ESV)

"And after you have suffered a little while, the God of all grace, who has called you to his eternal glory in Christ, will himself restore, confirm, strengthen, and establish you. To him be the dominion forever and ever. Amen."

Have you ever gotten the feeling that the things you were suffering were only because you're a child of God who's really trying to live the life you are called to live? You're not alone. In his first epistle, the apostle Peter wrote to the saints who were scattered in various places because of persecution. Believers were being martyred merely for their faith in Jesus Christ. Peter wrote to encourage them to keep their faith in Christ and that God would fulfil His Word toward them.

In case you haven't noticed, the last few days of this devotional book are complete with doxologies, expressions of praise to God which in turn bless the hearers. In today's doxology, Peter tells the persecuted saints that their suffering is seasonal, in so many words. It may seem like forever while you're in the midst of it, but when it's over, what lies ahead is so much more glorious. In Romans 8, Paul wrote, "for I reckon that the sufferings of this present day are not worthy to be compared to the glory that shall be revealed in us." What more to keep the Believer focused than to ensure him/her of God's promises of eternal glory? Peter doesn't just encourage the saints with thoughts of eternal glory, though. He wrote that God will Himself, "restore, confirm, strengthen, and establish" the saints. Let's look at these words to discover the blessings that await the Believer.

To "restore" in the Greek is to complete thoroughly. To "confirm" is to set fast or make stable. To "strengthen" is to do just that…to make one strong. To "establish" is to lay the foundation. To put all of these words together, especially for the Believer who is in an unstable, scary, and doubtful situation, God will build the Believer up to withstand any circumstance including death. It does not matter how shaky the environment around you is. *You* are lacking nothing. David said, "yea, though I walk through the valley of the shadow of death, I shall fear no evil; for Thou art with me…Thou preparest a table before me in the presence of mine enemies." Satan tries to make you doubt internally based on external circumstances. Trust The Lord, though. He's given you everything you need to keep that evil wolf from blowing your house down.

MY NOTES

Day 31

Hebrews 13:20-21 (ESV)

"Now may the God of peace who brought again from the dead our Lord Jesus, the great shepherd of the sheep, by the blood of the eternal covenant, equip you with everything good that you may do his will, working in us that which is pleasing in his sight, through Jesus Christ, to whom be glory forever and ever. Amen."

You've made it to the final day in this book. Congratulations! I'm celebrating with you, as it's the last day I'm writing (lol)! Today's encouragement is a mouth full and pretty much self-explanatory. Several days of this devotional book are dedicated to the benefits afforded to us by Jesus' substitutionary death on the cross. But just as many of our sermons close with getting Jesus up from the grave, this doxology will do the same! We know the Ghost Writer for the Book of Hebrews, but not the one who penned the letter. However, The Holy Ghost has packed blessing after blessing in this set of Scriptures.

Firstly, as Scripture records elsewhere, through Jesus we have peace with God. There is no more sin that separates us from God. Had Jesus still been in the grave, we would need another substitute to cleanse us from our sins. Jesus got up on the third day, though! Because He lives, He forever makes atonement for our sins. He, as the writer of Hebrews wrote, has saved us to the uttermost.

Even in light of this fact, though, some Believers still feel incomplete. The very fact that flaws still exist makes one feel they need "another dip" in the baptism pool or "more anointing." 2 Peter 1:3 tells us that God has "given unto us all things that pertain unto life and godliness," though, and he writes that this is revealed as we grow in knowledge of Christ. Jesus doesn't do half-jobs. What we need at the point of rebirth is given us perfectly. There are some things that need to happen in our spiritual development, though, to bring out what The Lord put in us. The writer of Hebrews writes that God grants the Believer the equipping of "everything good" so that we may do His Will. "Everything good"includes everything God knows we need to experience in order to excite the growth of the seed planted in us by The Spirit. God will give it to you if you do what Paul says in Romans 12. "And be not conformed to this world; but be ye transformed by the renewing of your mind, that ye may prove what is that good, and acceptable, and perfect, will of God." Growing in your knowledge of The Lord renews your mind and cultivates The Fruit of The Spirit in you.

Change is not going to happen just because you confessed Christ as your Lord and Savior. I know there have been many testimonies of habits being broken instantly at the point of regeneration, but the lifestyle is more than just breaking a habit or two. Sanctification and spiritual maturity are a lifetime process. Don't give up just because you're not where you think you need to be. May God grant you every good thing you need to produce the Fruit He desires to see in you.

Thank you for walking through The Word with me daily. It has been a joy praying and pouring into you. May God richly bless you and continue to inspire you through His Word. Amen.

MY NOTES